First published in Great Britain in 2018 by Wren & Rook
Text © Isabel Thomas, 2018
Illustrations © Alex Paterson, 2018
All rights reserved.

ISBN: 9781526361530
E-book ISBN: 9781526361523
10 9 8 7 6 5 4 3 2 1

Wren & Rook
An imprint of Hachette Children's Group
Part of Hodder & Stoughton
Carmelite House
50 Victoria Embankment
London EC4Y 0DZ
An Hachette UK Company
www.hachette.co.uk
www.hachettechildrens.co.uk

Printed in England

Publishing Director: Debbie Foy
Commissioning Editor: Elizabeth Brent
Art Director: Laura Hambleton

Designed by Thy Bui

Additional images supplied by Shutterstock

THIS BOOK IS NOT RUBBISH

ISABEL THOMAS
ILLUSTRATED BY ALEX PATERSON

wren
&rook

CONTENTS

1. **LIVING** ON THE **VEG!** 10

2. **DITCH** THE **WASHING UP** 16

3. **A BAN** ON **BATHS!** 22

4. **TURN BOTTLES** INTO **BOOMERANGS** 26

5. **PARTY** FOR THE **PLANET** 32

6. **DUMP** THE **GLITTER** 36

7. **EAT UGLY FOOD** 39

8. **SNACK** TO **SAVE** THE **WORLD** 42

9. **TURN TRASH** INTO **TREASURE** 46

10. **PLAN a RUBBISH DAY OUT** ... 48

11. **HAPPY BIRTHDAY ME PLANET!** 50

12. **SAY this is the LAST STRAW** 52

13. **THIS ROCK IS NOT RUBBISH** 56

14. **START a FIGHT at SCHOOL** 59

15. **MAKE a HEAP of RUBBISH** 62

16. **DON'T RUSH to FLUSH!** 66

17. **IT'S a WRAP** 70

18. **GO SWISHING** 72

19. **LET your GARDEN GET MESSY** 78

20. **SAVE** the **PLANET** while
you **SLEEP** 81

21. **DON'T HAND IN** your
HOMEWORK 84

22. **BE** a **BIRD BRAIN** 89

23. **USE** your **BUTT** 92

24. **BE** a **TREE HUGGER** 98

25. **CHALK IT UP** 104

26. **TAKE** a **BAG** for a **WALK** 108

27. **SAY NO THANK YOU' CARDS** .. 114

28. **EAT MORE CHIPS!** 118

29. **COTTON** on to
CLOTHES WASTE 120

30. **TAKE** your **JUNK** for
    a **HOT CHOCOLATE ...** 125

31. **MIND** the **GAP** 129

32. **THINK** like a **SEA TURTLE** 132

33. **GET ON** your **BIKE**
    (OR SKATES, OR SCOOTER ...) 136

34. **DRESS** to **IMPRESS** 140

35. **APPOINT YOURSELF**
    FAMILY CHIEF 142

36. **DESIGN** your **DREAM DEN** 146

37. **GO ROUND** and **ROUND**
    in **CIRCLES** 150

38. **START SHOUTING NOW!** 155

39. **ONLY LEAVE FOOTPRINTS** 160

40. **BE A CITIZEN SCIENTIST** 164

41. **DON'T BEE-LIEVE THE MYTHS** 168

42. **BECOME AN ART-ACTIVIST** 172

43. **DITCH THE SCHOOL RUN** 176

44. **READ THE LABEL (AND SAVE A RAINFOREST)** 180

45. **CACHE IN** 184

46. **GAME OVER** 188

47. **GET A GREEN PET** 192

48. **EAT SLOW** 196

49. **SCRUB YOURSELF GREEN** 201

50. **GET RID OF THIS BOOK** 204

QUICK GUIDE TO THE

PLANET-O-METER

SAVES:

WILDLIFE

PAPER/WOOD

ELECTRICITY

LITTER/LANDFILL

PLASTIC

RAINFOREST

RECYCLING

CARBON FOOTPRINT

POLLUTION

WATER

FOOD

IMPACT: **COST:**   **DIFFICULTY:**

LIVING ON THE VEG!

When it comes to gobbling up resources, meaty meals are the planet's number one enemy. Going veggie for one day each week can make a BIG difference.

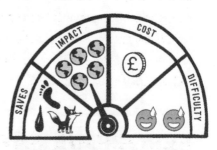

PLANET-O-METER

Every year, 7.6 billion humans chomp their way through meat from an amazing 65 billion animals. Raising these animals – and getting them from the farm to your burger bun – puts pressure on the planet in three ways.

HELP!

BAA BAA LAND

Most of the world's farmland – and almost a third of all usable land – is devoted to raising animals for meat and milk. It's not just fields of grass playing home to cows and sheep: almost a third of the crops we grow are used to feed animals, too. This farmland has replaced forests and destroyed natural habitats.

FEROCIOUS FARTS

Livestock emit the same amount of greenhouse gases as all the fossil-fuel-guzzling vehicles in the world! Cows are the **WORST** culprits.

As they digest grass, they constantly burp and fart methane, one of the most harmful greenhouse gases. Each of the 1.5 billion cattle on the planet can expel up to 500 litres of methane in a day!

WATER WORRIES

Looking after all those animals accounts for nearly 10 per cent of all the freshwater humans use each year. Even more water is used to keep meat clean and cool, on its journey from field to fork. Animal farming is also one of the main sources of water pollution, because animal poo and other chemicals wash into rivers and oceans.

Scientists have crunched the numbers and calculated the carbon footprints of the nation's favourite meaty meals ...

Half a leg of lamb

39.2 kg of carbon dioxide, or **150 km** in an average car.

Four large beef burgers

27 kg of carbon dioxide, or **105 km** in an average car.

20 pork sausages

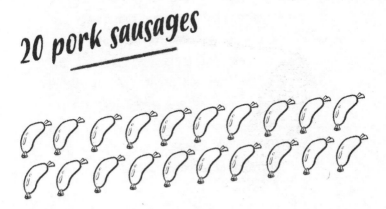

12.1 kg of carbon dioxide, or **50 km** in an average car.

If you and your family avoid meat (and cheese too) for just one day a week, it could help the planet more than taking your family car off the road for **FIVE WEEKS**.

What about the other six days? Well, if you love meat too much to go veggie but you want to be kinder to the environment, stick with chicken, and fish that's caught in a responsible way. Eggs are an even greener source of animal protein (but DON'T eat them if they actually are green ...).

By 2050, at least 9 BILLION people will be sharing our planet (50 years ago there were just 3.5 billion). It's not possible for all those people to feast on beef and lamb. Meat protein will HAVE to come from different sources. Some of the ideas scientists are working on include 'cultured meat' grown in labs, and protein from insects! That bean burger's starting to look pretty good now, isn't it?!

DITCH THE WASHING UP

You hate it, and the planet hates it too! Happily, putting less effort into doing the dishes is a win-win situation.

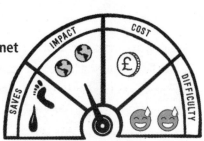

PLANET-O-METER

Have you ever fancied taking part in some scientific research? Scientists are always looking for people to help test their theories. **BUT BE CAREFUL WHAT YOU VOLUNTEER FOR**. The unlucky participants in one scientific study were asked to wash 144 dirty dishes, pots, pans and pieces of cutlery – **EACH**! It did have a purpose though. The study found that people approached the task in very different ways – some much kinder to the environment than others.

Washing the dishes uses around 5 per cent of **ALL** water we use at home. A typical household washes dishes by hand 10 times a week, using **30 LITRES** if the washing or rinsing is done under a running tap. It's possible to use much less water if you avoid wasteful habits like running the hot tap to rinse dishes. Every minute, a running tap pours out 8 to 12 litres of water – a week's worth of drinking water.

Heating this water releases the equivalent of **8 kg** of carbon dioxide – that's as much as if you left a 42-inch LCD TV on for **48 hours**.

COUNTDOWN TO ECO-FRIENDLY WASHING UP

5. Scrape as much leftover food as possible into the compost bin (see pages 62–65).

4. Run a basin of warm (not hot) water – and only when you have a full load of dishes to wash.

3. Wash glasses and cutlery first. Then wash dirtier dishes. Pile the soapy dishes up on the draining board.

2. Run half a basin of cold water. Dip the soapy dishes in for a rinse.

1. Leave the dishes to dry naturally in the air.

If your family uses a dishwasher, you'll be **VERY** pleased to hear they can be kinder to the planet – as long as you don't rinse the dishes first. A typical dishwasher cycle only uses 12–15 litres of water, but pre-rinsing dishes under the tap can waste a shocking 22,000 litres of water each year! Instead, scrape any leftovers into your compost caddy (see pages 62–65). Some modern smart dishwashers can sense how dirty dishes are, and adjust their settings accordingly.

For extra eco-points, always make sure the dishwasher is completely full, use the coolest cycle possible, and run the dishwasher in the middle of the night to make the most of greener electricity (see pages 81–83). Save the planet while you sleep (and don't ruin your good work by arguing about whose turn it is to unload it!).

Did you know that drying up is bad for you? And no, not just because it's boring! One scientific study found that 89 per cent of tea towels are harbouring bacteria from poo. BLEURGH. In a quarter of cases this included E. coli bacteria, which can cause nasty stomach bugs. Throw in the (tea) towel, and save water and energy on laundry too.

A BAN ON BATHS!

Want to know why the bathroom is a battleground for eco-warriors?

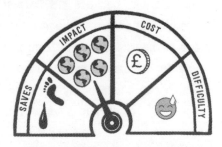

PLANET-O-METER

One of the top ways to cut the volume of greenhouse gases belched into the air by our houses is to reduce the amount of water we heat up at home. In Japan, for example, supplying and heating water for homes causes 5 per cent of all carbon dioxide emissions, and 60 per cent of this goes on hot-water bathing. Skipping even one bath each week can make a **BIG** difference. Swap it for a shower so you don't get too stinky.

If you already prefer showers, don't be too smug. Fast-flowing and rainfall shower heads use up to 17 litres of water per minute, meaning that an average eight-minute shower can use almost double the energy and water of a bath!

To make showers more eco-friendly, time yourself and get out after five minutes. Use a waterproof watch or a wind-up egg timer (remember, no mains electricity in the bathroom). Encourage your family to take the five-minute shower challenge too and you could save thousands of litres of hot water – and hundreds of pounds – every year.

Banning baths and taking speedy showers isn't the only way to save water in the bathroom. You can be an eco-warrior every time you use the sink and loo. Brushing your teeth for two minutes uses about 10 litres of water each time (that's 20 litres per day if you brush twice a day – which you do, don't you?!). If you turn the tap off whilst brushing, you'll save a lot of water. If you usually run a tap while you wash your face or hands, run a small sink of water instead and save an extra 12 litres!

TURN THE TAP OFF!

Each person in the UK uses an average of 142 litres of clean water every day. A quarter of this – the biggest single chunk – goes on showers.

TURN BOTTLES INTO BOOMERANGS

If you haven't heard how bad plastic water bottles are by now, you've been living on a different planet … one that's not being choked by a giant floating garbage patch.

More than 480 **BILLION** plastic bottles are sold around the world every year, adding up to a planet-sized problem. Placed end to end, these bottles would circle the world around 1,870 times … and that's almost exactly what's happening. Each year, millions of tonnes of plastic litter makes it way to the oceans, where it collects in gigantic, floating garbage patches.

PLANET-O-METER

Plastic's greatest strength – being almost indestructible – is also its greatest problem. While paper or cardboard rot away in weeks, plastic bottles take at least **450 YEARS** to wear down. And even then, plastic doesn't decompose completely – it just breaks into smaller and smaller pieces. The United Nations has warned that these tiny pieces, called 'microplastics', are doing irreparable damage to the creatures that live in seas and oceans.

In the minute it took you to read this far, **1 MILLION** plastic bottles have been bought, beginning a journey that all-too-often ends in the stomachs of zooplankton, fish, albatross chicks, whales and seals.

Whether you're puffing and panting on the sports pitch, sweating through the school disco or crying tears of boredom in a grammar lesson, you need to drink all day long to replace the water your body uses. But this doesn't have to come from a disposable plastic bottle. After all, PET (the plastic used for most soft drinks and water bottles) wasn't invented until the 1970s, and at least 100 billion people had managed not to die of dehydration before then! Plastic is just a bad habit, and it's up to us all to break it.

So, what can you do? Here are some ideas. Invest in a bottle that's easy to clean and reuse. Write your name on it, so it comes back to you, like a boomerang! Fill it up before you go out for the day, and while you're on the move, look out for water fountains or ask at a café or restaurant if you can top up. And if you find yourself filling up your water bottle in a coffee shop while the adults around you clutch disposable coffee cups with disposable plastic lids, be sure to bring out your best hard stare.

**2.5 billion coffee cups are used and
thrown away each year in the UK.**

If you do end up with a disposable plastic bottle, it's not the end of
the world (well, not yet) – make sure you reuse it as many times as
possible before finding a recycling bin. Keep an eye out for deposit
return schemes too – in some places you can even make money by
collecting discarded bottles and bringing them to be recycled.

Since plastic was invented in the early 1900s, about 8.3 billion tonnes has been produced ... and about 6.3 billion tonnes of this has been thrown away. Only 9 per cent has been recycled. The rest is sitting in landfills or elsewhere in the environment, quietly not rotting away. If we don't want a plastic planet, we need to take action now.

By 2050, the plastic in the world's oceans
will weigh more than all the fish.

PARTY FOR THE PLANET

Each birthday is a celebration that you've made one more trip around the Sun ... so why not plan a party to look after the planet that gave you a ride?

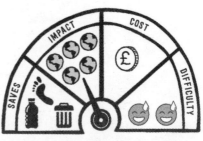

PLANET-O-METER

Parties are awesome, but for the planet they're no cause for celebration. Birthdays only come once a year, so most party goods are disposable. Wrapping paper, cards, decorations, paper plates and napkins, plastic cups and cutlery are all designed to be used for a few hours and thrown away. But it doesn't have to be this way.

COUNTDOWN TO AN ECO-FRIENDLY PARTY

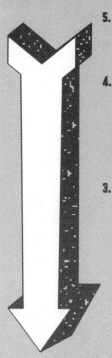

5. Send your invitations and thank-you cards by email.

4. Make your own bunting by sticking triangles of used wrapping paper, comics or scrap fabric to a piece of string or raffia.

3. Serve food and drinks using washable plates, cups and cutlery. You might be able to pick up a whole set second-hand for less than the price of disposables! Keep them in a special box between parties and lend them out to friends and family, too.

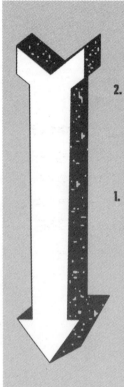

2. No napkins! Provide a bowl of soapy water and a towel instead. Set out small compost and recycling bins to make sure rubbish ends up in the right place.

I. Instead of filling plastic party bags with plastic toys, get your guests to make a gift to take home. How about decorating a clay plant pot, sciencing up some slime, or creating your own cupcakes?

Americans are some of the biggest fans of plastic knives, forks and spoons, using an estimated 40 billion per year. France has already passed a law banning single-use plastic cups, cutlery and plates. From 2020, only compostable items will be allowed.

DUMP THE GLITTER

Glitter – so shiny, so sparkly, so pretty ... AND SO DEADLY!

PLANET-O-METER

Glitter is made out of tiny pieces of reflective foil coated with coloured plastic. From clothes to cosmetics to craft kits, it's never been more popular. But for eco-heroes, it's definitely lost its sparkle.

Anyone who's used glitter knows that the tiny flakes get **EVERYWHERE**. Receive one sparkly card, and you're washing it out of your hair, carpet and dog for weeks. But have you thought about where the glitter goes once you wash it down the sink? Straight through water filtration systems and into the oceans, where it can do terrible damage to the creatures that live there (see page 134).

These tiny plastic particles are also making their way back to our plates. Hundreds of marine animals eat plastic (in the ocean, plastic particles quickly become covered with a layer of algae that makes them smell delicious to fish). This means that every time we eat fish or seafood, we're also eating microplastics or chemicals that have leaked out of them. Being a vegetarian doesn't help either – plastic fibres have been found in sea salt, and even in honey. No one knows yet what the impact will be on human health. Glitter doesn't seem so pretty now, does it?

Some people have called for glitter to be banned, but there is a glimmer of light at the end of the tunnel. Scientists are researching biodegradable glitter made from natural materials such as eucalyptus instead of plastic. So if you can't resist a bit of sparkle in your face paint, bath bombs or craft supplies, try to track down this 'eco-glitter'. Or you could follow the lead of one group of nurseries in the UK and try using lentils instead (although maybe not on your face …).

Scientists think that between 15 and
51 TRILLION microplastic particles have
already made their way into the oceans.

EAT UGLY FOOD

Be an eco-superhero in the supermarket by playing the ugly food game. Who can track down (and take home) the strangest-looking fruit and veg?

PLANET-0-METER

Time to get (even more) serious for a minute: 815 million people – 1 in 10 of the world's population – don't have enough to eat, and undernutrition is causing the deaths of more than 3 million children every year. But the problem is not that the planet can't produce enough food to feed everyone. Shockingly, a **THIRD** of the food produced every year gets thrown away.

Time to GET SERIOUS.

The waste happens in many different places – on farms, where crops that don't look perfect are left to rot; in supermarkets, where 'ugly' fruit and veg aren't put out on display or are left on the shelves by shoppers; and in our homes, where food is forgotten at the back of the fridge until it's too mouldy and disgusting to eat. In the US, around 14 per cent of all rubbish sent to landfills is food that has been thrown away.

Our shopping, cooking and eating habits are a big part of the problem. But this means we have the power to be part of the solution too! Each time you help with food shopping, make it your mission to find the ugliest fruits and vegetables you can. No item is too blemished, big, small or gnarly – if they're on the shelf, they're safe to eat. Give them a home so they don't get thrown away – they'll still taste delicious!

In the UK, 7.3 million tonnes of household food waste was thrown away in 2015. That's enough to feed everyone in a city the size of London for a year! Around 4.4 million tonnes of this was 'avoidable' waste, such as bread that went mouldy or milk that went off before anyone got around to eating or drinking it.

SNACK TO SAVE THE WORLD

Billions of people who, like us, are lucky enough to live in houses with plugs and light switches treat electricity a bit like air ... it's invisible and always available, so we don't think about how much we use.

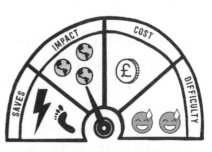

PLANET-O-METER

It's really easy to forget where electricity comes from. After all, tablets and TVs don't belch out smoke and soot. But the dirty truth is that most of the energy used to generate electricity still comes from burning fossil fuel – an eco-warrior's arch enemy.

Burning coal, oil or natural gas releases huge volumes of gases such as carbon dioxide, which increase the natural 'greenhouse effect' of Earth's atmosphere. The result? A planet that's heating up, leading to long-term climate change. The bad news is that this will cause a rise in sea levels, severe flooding, extreme weather, drought, extinction of many species, food shortages and the spread of diseases. There is no good news. And all because we love the convenience of energy on demand.

Governments and the energy industry are exploring alternative energy sources, but in the meantime we can all help by trying to use less electricity.

TOP ECO-TIPS FOR ZAPPING YOUR ELECTRICITY USE

5 Open your curtains or blinds first thing in the morning instead of reaching for the light switch. Turn lights off when you leave a room (unless someone else is still in it, of course!).

4 Don't leave the fridge door open when you're foraging for your next snack. Up to 7 per cent of an appliance's total energy use goes on cooling down the warmer air that rushes in when the door is opened.

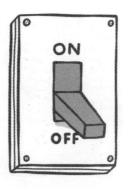

3 Fridges use less energy if they are two-thirds full. If your fridge is overcrowded, start munching to save the planet!

2 When you use devices with screens, turn the volume off and the brightness down so they need charging less often.

1 Don't leave TVs, computers and consoles on standby overnight. The lazy way to do this is to plug them into a timer device, which will do the remembering for you.

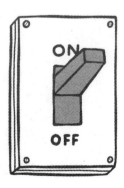

TURN TRASH INTO TREASURE

Do you ever dream of finding buried treasure and making your fortune? Try digging in your recycling box!

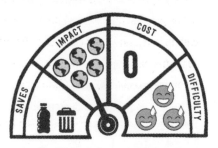

PLANET-O-METER

It might look like rubbish and smell like rubbish, but to someone else, it's just what they were looking for. Many people, from artists to teachers, need household materials to use in craft projects. Go on a scavenger hunt for the following items:

- ☆ loo roll and kitchen roll tubes
- ☆ egg boxes
- ☆ empty glass jars and perfume bottles
- ☆ old buttons
- ☆ bent coat hangers
- ☆ scraps of fabric
- ☆ pine cones
- ☆ corks from bottles

- ⭐ ring pulls from cans
- ⭐ plastic milk bottle tops
- ⭐ metal bottle tops

Once you've built up a collection, ask your parents to sell it for you online using a 'pre-loved' or auction site. Your junk will be less likely to end up in a landfill and could even be turned into something beautiful. To go the extra mile for the environment, donate the proceeds to your favourite eco charity, or use it to 'adopt' an endangered animal.

BE SURE TO FOLLOW THESE RULES:

Only collect clean, safe items, in good condition.

Ask an adult to do the selling and sending for you. Don't use online selling websites yourself.

Collect used packaging material, then reuse it to pack up and send your items.

PLAN A RUBBISH DAY OUT ...

… and find out where your garbage goes.

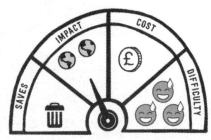

PLANET-O-METER

Imagine if your family stopped putting the bins out and stored all your rubbish at home instead. It would soon get pretty stinky. Think the smelliest cheese, mixed with rotten eggs and your trainers after sports day (OK, maybe not **THAT** bad). After a year, you'd be wading through more than a **TONNE** of packaging and food waste – the average for households in the UK.

We're super lucky that our waste gets taken away every week or every fortnight, but it means we never get to see how much waste we really produce. While you can't really start stockpiling it in your bedroom, you can do the next best thing. Find out where your garbage goes once you've waved goodbye to the bin lorry.

Many landfill and recycling sites offer free tours for individuals or groups. If your family doesn't fancy it, ask your school if they could organise a trip. You'll learn what happens to waste in your area, and what steps you can take to reduce the amount you throw away. You might even see high-tech rubbish robots sorting materials and making bales. And once you've seen the scale of a stinking landfill site, you'll **DEFINITELY** be inspired to reduce, reuse and recycle like never before. Plus your bedroom will look **REALLY** tidy in comparison!

HAPPY BIRTHDAY ~~ME~~ PLANET

Next time you're writing your birthday list, include a present for the planet, too!

PLANET-O-METER

People **LOVE** to give presents – even more then they like receiving them! (OK, there are exceptions …) It's so hardwired into us that you can go anywhere in the world and find people giving gifts to strengthen bonds with family and friends. Scientists who study gift-giving (surely one of the most awesome jobs on the planet #jobgoals) have found that the perfect gift is not the most expensive one – it's a gift that someone has actually asked for. So let's start asking for stuff that has the power to save the planet!

> The **PERFECT GIFT** is something that someone has actually asked for!

Instead of more 'stuff', ask for activities or planet-friendly gifts such as:

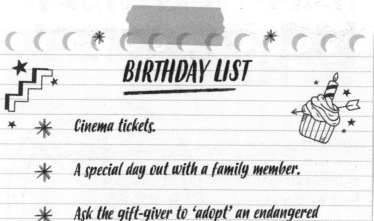

BIRTHDAY LIST

* Cinema tickets.

* A special day out with a family member.

* Ask the gift-giver to 'adopt' an endangered animal on your behalf.

* Let friends and family know that you're happy to receive pre-loved gifts, such as a great piece of clothing, or a book that they've read and enjoyed.

* Or ask for a gift card that you can spend on something you really need, rather than a present that might go to waste.

There's always that one relative who will ignore your birthday list and get you a book that's not as good as this one, or a jumper that laughs in the face of fashion. Put gifts you don't like or can't use to one side, and re-gift them later. Then you can be an eco-friendly gift-giver too!

SAY THIS IS LAST STRAW
THE

They're completely unnecessary and wreaking havoc on ocean wildlife. It's time to ditch the straws!

People in the UK use around 8.5 billion drinking straws every year. Each one gets used for just a few minutes before it's thrown away, and like all plastic litter, straws often end up in the ocean where they take more than 200 **YEARS** to break down. In fact, straws are one of

PLANET-O-METER

the top 10 items found in beach clean-ups – and that's the best-case scenario. Plastic straws have been found lodged in the nostrils of sea turtles and tangled in the stomachs of penguins. You get the picture – straws suck.

Up to 90 per cent of the world's seabirds have plastic in their guts.

Some cities and countries have already banned plastic straws, and more will follow suit. The fun-suckers may be replaced by more eco-friendly alternatives, including straws made from paper, straws made from metal and even straws made from straw! This is not actually a new idea – in the past, the very first drinking straws were the hollow stalks of plants! They were replaced by paper that was waxed to make it waterproof, and eventually by plastic. Several companies are reintroducing biodegradable, compostable straws, but these still have to be manufactured and transported to shops and homes, sucking up resources on the way. The best action is to say no to straws altogether.

THIS ROCK IS NOT RUBBISH

Forget about fidget spinners, loom bands, slime and Pokémon. The biggest craze sweeping the planet is painted pebbles!

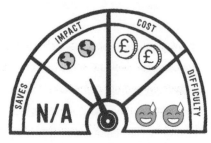

PLANET-O-METER

Look carefully when you're out and about, and you might spot a rock that doesn't look like all the others. Rocks painted with bright pictures and patterns have been popping up all over the country in all sorts of places – in parks, behind bushes, under trees and on beaches.

Many have a message on the back, encouraging the finder to share a picture of the rock on social media, before re-hiding it or painting their own.

Why not start your own rock-painting scheme, with an eco-message? Seek out some rocks or pebbles and decorate them with waterproof paints (avoid spray paints, which are not kind to the planet). On the bottom of each rock, include an eco-tip and the hashtag **#ThisRockIsNotRubbish**. Hide the rocks in your local area, then spread the word. When people find a rock, they will be able to look up the hashtag and see even more eco-tips!

ECO ~~WORRIERS~~ WARRIORS

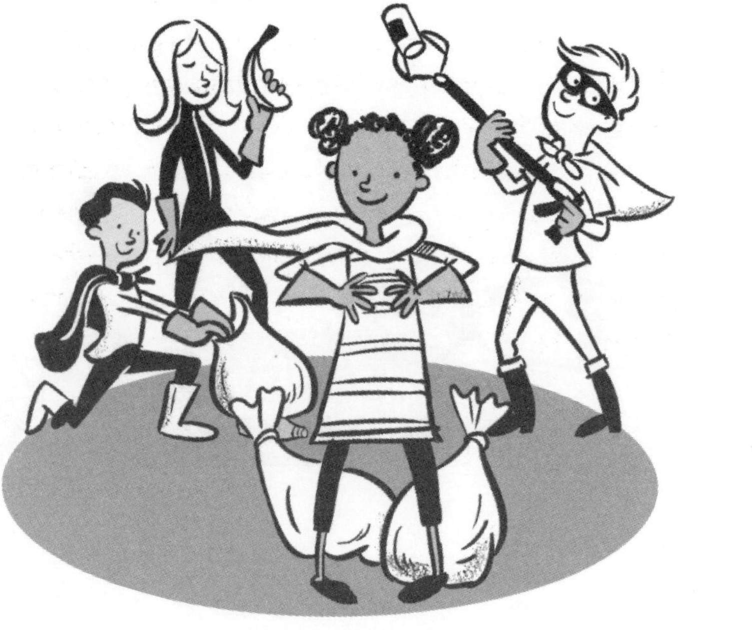

START A FIGHT AT SCHOOL

Be an eco-warrior, not an eco-worrier.

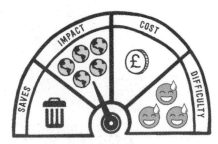

PLANET-O-METER

Team up with some like-minded classmates and set up a school Eco Squad. It's a great way to multiply your planet-saving efforts **AND** spend more time with your friends. Think of yourselves as the eco-Avengers! Plan a term's worth of activities and ask a teacher if they will lend a hand. If you can't start a club, why not ask a member of your School Council to suggest similar actions? Or plan a school assembly to share your ideas and inspire your whole school to play their part in saving the planet.

10 IDEAS TO KICK-START YOUR ECO SQUAD

1 Form a litter-picking team to fight rubbish in your local area.

2 Plant a wildflower meadow at school.

3 Transform junk into gifts to sell at your school fair.

4 Make posters to encourage people to cycle or walk to school.

5 Start a #ThisRockIsNotRubbish project (see pages 56–57).

6 Carry out a green audit to find out how much your school is already doing to save the planet.

7 Build a giant bug hotel using old wooden pallets and natural materials.

8 Hang home-made bird feeders in the school grounds (see pages 89–91).

9 Share paper-saving and recycling ideas (see pages 142–145) next to every photocopier, bin and resources cupboard.

10 Set up a vegetable garden in the school grounds.

MAKE A HEAP OF RUBBISH

Starting a compost heap is an easy way to harness the planet's own recycling power!

PLANET-O-METER

A compost heap is basically a massive pile of rubbish. Or, if you want to be fancy, 'organic waste'. You can chuck almost anything that used to be alive on it, from fruit peel, stale bread and egg shells to grass clippings, paper and cardboard. You can even compost your hair clippings! Putting it all in one big heap speeds up the natural chemical reactions that recycle dead stuff into the ingredients for new life. Compost heaps also provide a toasty warm home for animals that are very much alive, including earthworms, slugs, snails, millipedes, slow-worms and even grass snakes. It's basically a free ticket to your very own minibeast safari park!

Once the compost is ready, it helps plants grow more quickly and easily. Unlike shop-bought fertilisers or mulch, home-made compost is free! It also comes without plastic packaging or the energy cost of transporting it to your home. It turns out compost is not rubbish at all!

COUNTDOWN
TO CREATING YOUR
OWN COMPOST

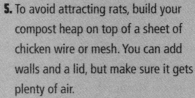

5. To avoid attracting rats, build your compost heap on top of a sheet of chicken wire or mesh. You can add walls and a lid, but make sure it gets plenty of air.

4. Keep a little bin in the kitchen especially for food scraps, and empty it straight on to your compost heap. This means less food waste goes in the bin.

3. Keep meat, oil and cheese out of the compost heap to avoid attracting nasty pests.

2. You can put pet litter on the compost heap, but only if your pet is vegetarian.

1. When the waste has become crumbly compost, it can be scattered all over the garden, or mixed into the soil you use for house plants.

DON'T RUSH TO FLUSH!

How often do you flush the toilet? In a survey, 63 per cent of people said they flush after every wee. Science says this is too often.

PLANET-O-METER

Over a quarter of the water we use at home goes straight down the toilet! Researchers at Indiana University in the US have shown that flushing less often could reduce our water usage and bills much more quickly than turning off the tap while brushing our teeth, or even taking shorter showers (see page 23) can.

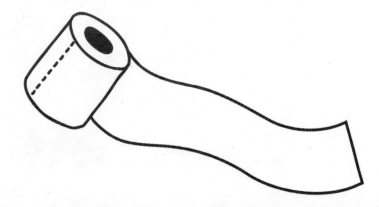

If it's yellow, let it mellow

OFFICIALLY BACKED BY SCIENCE!

If your family aren't convinced, there are other things you can do. If you have an older, larger cistern, ask if you can pop in a brick or an air-filled bag that stops the cistern filling with more water than needed. Some water companies provide these 'hippos' for free, and they can save more than a day's worth of drinking water **PER FLUSH**.

Even easier is taking your first wee of the day in the shower! This was the focus of recent campaigns in Brazil and the UK. Urine is totally germ-free, so as long as the water is flowing, it's perfectly clean. And it's all headed for the same place anyway: the sewers. Doing just one daily wee in the shower could save 2,500 litres of water in a year – enough to fill a hot tub! (Though we definitely don't recommend doing that – the hot tub is another eco-enemy!)

Don't worry about adding too much extra time to your shower, either. Humans only take an average of 21 seconds to do a wee!

IT'S A WRAP

If you've planned the perfect eco-friendly gift, don't ruin all your good work by covering it in sheets of wrapping paper that will be ripped off in seconds and never used again.

PLANET-O-METER

In the UK, we throw away 400,000 km of wrapping paper at Christmas alone – enough to wrap the planet (around the equator) **TEN** times. Stuffing it into the recycling bin doesn't undo the damage. Most wrapping paper contains inks, plastic film, foil and glitter, not to mention sticky tape, so it can't be recycled. Try one of these ideas instead:

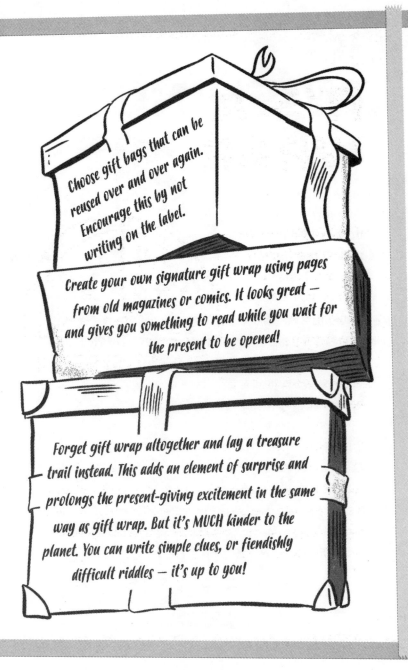

Choose gift bags that can be reused over and over again. Encourage this by not writing on the label.

Create your own signature gift wrap using pages from old magazines or comics. It looks great — and gives you something to read while you wait for the present to be opened!

Forget gift wrap altogether and lay a treasure trail instead. This adds an element of surprise and prolongs the present-giving excitement in the same way as gift wrap. But it's MUCH kinder to the planet. You can write simple clues, or fiendishly difficult riddles — it's up to you!

GO SWISHING

A swish – or clothes-swapping party – is a fun and free way to update your wardrobe without putting a strain on the planet.

PLANET-O-METER

High-street shops are full of cheap, disposable clothes – and so are landfill sites. WRAP (the UK's Waste and Resources Action Programme) has done some detective work and discovered that fashion is environmental enemy number four, after housing, transport and food (which are probably harder to give up!).

**IN THE UK, WE BUY MORE THAN
A MILLION TONNES OF CLOTHING EVERY YEAR.
THAT'S HARD TO PICTURE BUT IMAGINE THIS …**

☆ 22,727 articulated lorry-loads of cotton, nylon and sequins.

Producing and then washing all these clothes …

☆ releases as much carbon dioxide into the atmosphere
as the entire countries of Afghanistan and Zimbabwe do
put together

☆ uses enough water to fill every bath in the UK every day
for 10 years.

For every single tonne of clothing made, another 1.7 tonnes of waste is left behind. On top of this, 300,000 tonnes of clothing – worth £140 million – are sent to landfills every year.

To make sure our passion for fashion doesn't keep on stripping the planet of resources, we need to love and value our clothes more. This means keeping them out of landfills by carrying out small repairs, wearing the same item more often and giving clothes a longer life – even if that's in someone else's wardrobe. One of the easiest ways to do this is to swish …

SWISH …

In the UK, three-quarters of us throw away unwanted clothes rather than recycling or donating them.

SWISH ...

COUNTDOWN TO A SWISH

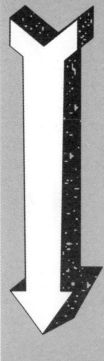

5. Choose a date and time. Send an e-invite to friends who like similar clothes. Ask them to gather clothes and accessories that they no longer wear or use, but are in good, clean condition.

4. As people arrive, swap their donations for tokens. You could use cardboard counters.

3. Display all the donations for everyone to browse. Why not put out some drinks and snacks too?

2. When you're ready, draw straws (not plastic ones!) to decide who goes first. Take it in turns to swap your tokens for 'new-to-you' items.

1. If anything is left over, donate it to a local charity shop.

You don't have to only Swish clothes. Include accessories, books, sports gear or toys — anything that you've grown bored of but once loved.

LET YOUR GARDEN GET MESSY

When it comes to gardening, less is more …

PLANET-O-METER

There's nothing wildlife hates more than a neatly mown lawn. Lock up the lawnmower, ditch the weeding and let the (leaf) litter pile up.

COUNTDOWN TO A REALLY WILD GARDEN

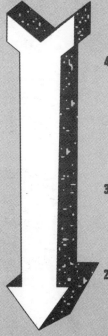

5. Stop mowing an area of grass over summer, and let it grow long. Even 1 square metre will let wildflowers grow and give small animals a place to hide.

4. Instead of cultivated flowers (which often contain little nectar and pollen) scatter native wildflower seeds to create a meadow border. You'll attract insects, which in turn will attract birds and bats.

3. Make small holes under walls and fences so animals can pass easily from garden to garden.

2. Don't tidy up fallen leaves and dead wood. Piles of leaves, twigs or logs are cosy homes for hibernating animals.

1. Dig a small pond and turn an ordinary garden into a wildlife haven!

SAVE THE PLANET WHILE YOU SLEEP

More electricity than ever before is being generated from renewable sources, including solar, wind, biomass and hydropower. However, there's still a long way to go ...

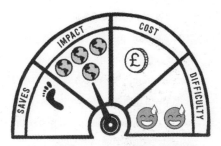

PLANET-O-METER

Most of this 'green' electricity can only be generated when it's sunny or windy. At times of high demand – like the tea break after a nail-biting penalty shootout – only fossil-fuel-burning, greenhouse-gas-belching power stations can deal with the surge in demand.

You can help by refusing to do any chores that involve electricity ... but only at peak times! Save your chores for times of low demand instead. Ditto for devices that run on mains electricity. Make sure they're not left on standby during times of peak demand.

In general, the late afternoon and early evening are times of peak power demand, when people come home from school and work and switch on lights, kettles, TVs and ovens. We generally use less electricity at night when most people are asleep. This is a good time to run washing machines and dishwashers, and to charge devices such as tablets and mobile phones. In the future, 'smart' devices that can collect and share data with each other (known as the 'internet of things') will probably make these decisions for us. In the meantime, you can find out the best and worst times of day to use electricity at:

WWF.ORG.UK/UPDATES/HOW-DO-YOU-MAKE-GREEN-CUP-TEA

or ask your electricity supplier.

It might seem like a small change, but if enough families follow this advice, it could mean fewer new power stations will need to be built!

Around a quarter of electricity generated around the world comes from renewable sources.

DON'T HAND IN YOUR HOMEWORK ...

... email it instead! When it comes to schoolwork, tell your teacher that more screen time actually could save the planet.

More than 400 million tonnes of paper are produced each year – the equivalent of 230 loo rolls for everyone on the planet. Of course, it's not all loo roll. Around a quarter is printing and writing paper. Making this paper involves cutting down 4 billion trees each year, and trees may be renewable, but the energy, water and chemicals involved in making paper gives it a hefty carbon footprint.

PLANET-O-METER

One easy way to cut down on the paper we use is to stop wasting it. The average UK family throws away six trees' worth of paper every year, while in the USA, a billion trees' worth of paper ends up in the bin each year. About two-thirds of paper is recycled, which is great, but paper is still one of the most common waste items in landfills.

Paper is also the main type of waste created by schools in the UK. We need paper in schools – to share ideas, practise new skills and be creative. But saving the planet means finding different ways to work. Try some of these ideas:

☆ Suggest that your teacher sends letters and sets homework via email.

☆ Ask if you can do your homework digitally and email it to your teacher.

☆ Use a little whiteboard for making notes and drafts.

☆ Rather than photocopying something, take a photograph and store it digitally.

☆ Always use both sides of the paper, and finish an exercise book before starting a new one.

Use a whiteboard!

☆ Set up a scrap paper drawer in each classroom, and recycle any paper that can't be used as scrap.

☆ Think before you print ... can you read it on screen?

☆ Only print the page or section you need.

☆ Set your printer default to double-sided printing.

☆ Reuse old drawings and drafts as wrapping paper (after all, it's the thought that counts ...).

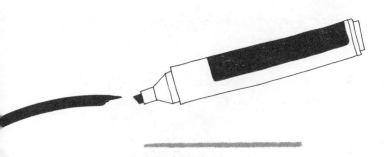

The pulp and paper industry is the fifth-largest consumer of energy in the world. It makes up 4 per cent of the world's total energy consumption!

BE A BIRD BRAIN

Where have all the insects gone? You're not the only one wondering. Birds rely on creepy-crawlies for every meal.

PLANET-O-METER

Once upon a time, every long car drive would end with a windscreen splattered with insects that were flying in the wrong place at the wrong time. Today's cars tend to stay much cleaner, which is good news if you're responsible for washing the car, but terrible news for the planet.

A large-scale study has shown that the number of insects in Europe is falling fast. In 1989, 17,291 hover flies were caught in traps from just one German nature reserve. In 2014, the same traps collected just 2,737 flies. Habitat loss, changes in land use and the chemicals that farms pour on to fields are partly to blame. This isn't just bad news for the insects, either. Many other animals – especially birds – rely on creepy-crawlies for food.

You can give birds a helping hand by putting up a bird feeder in your garden. Even better news? It's easy to make one from junk – another way to help the planet! Here are two ways to make your own – ask an adult to help you:

1

1 Poke two or three holes straight through a clean empty plastic bottle.

2 Balance an old wooden spoon through each pair of holes.

3 Widen the holes above the hollow of each spoon a little.

4 Fill the bottle with bird seed and replace the lid.

5 Hang from the branch of a tree.

1 Cut a hole in the side of a clean empty plastic milk bottle.

2 Poke a small hole just underneath the larger hole, to hold a little stick or pencil.

3 Fill the base with bird seed and replace the lid. Hang from the branch of a tree.

USE YOUR BUTT

It's not a rainy day – it's a free water day! Here's how to make the most of it.

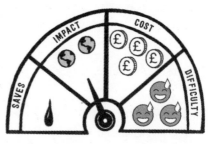

PLANET-O-METER

It might not feel like it when your visit to the BMX track is rained off for the fourth day in a row, but fresh water is a precious and scarce resource. More than 97 per cent of Earth's water is salty, and while

it looks lovely from space, it's doesn't help quench the thirst of the 6.5 million species of plants and animals that live on land.

We can only drink the remaining 2.5 per cent – or 10.6 million km^3 – of freshwater. This sounds like a lot, but if you think of it as 10 glasses full of water:

Almost seven are frozen as snow and ice .... ❄

More than three are hidden away underground .... ⬇

Leaving just a few drops of water which are found in lakes, swamps, rivers, reservoirs and streams ... . 🚰

... and we all have to share it.

Around half of the world's population already lives in areas where there isn't enough water. And even in countries where it rains a lot (like the UK – sigh), the water supply is often stretched in the summer. This makes water one of the world's most precious resources.

Every drop you can save helps. Even better, invest in a water butt and harvest this liquid gold for free!

COUNTDOWN TO WATER CONSERVATION

5. A water butt is the easiest way to collect loads of rainwater. Check that you're allowed to fit one in your area. They usually come with kits to collect all the water running down a drainpipe.

4. Make sure your butt has a lid to stop animals or small children falling in. Add a teaspoon of vegetable oil to sit on the surface and stop mosquitoes or midges breeding.

3. Plants don't need water that has been treated to make it safe for humans to drink. Rainwater can actually be better for them. Fill a water pistol and give your house plants a good soaking.

2. Use rainwater to wash the car, or even flush the toilet!

1. Don't drink the water you collect or use it for water fights.

100,000 litres of rainwater fall on
to the average roof EACH YEAR!
And most goes straight into sewers.

BE A TREE HUGGER

For immediate eco-impact, you can't do better than planting a tree. And if you can't plant one, adopt one!

PLANET-O-METER

Trees are the biggest plants on the planet, and vital for life as we know it. As they photosynthesise (make food for themselves, using the energy in sunlight) they soak up the greenhouse gas carbon dioxide, trapping it in their trunks, branches, roots and leaves. The only waste product is oxygen, the gas that keeps every other creature alive. How amazing is that?!

Tree canopies improve the air in other ways too, catching dust and dangerous pollutants which are then washed away by rain. They protect habitats from soil erosion, floods and drought – and provide habitats for millions of other living things.

For hundreds of thousands of years, trees have provided the materials for human shelter, tools and fire. For medicines, musical instruments and furniture. For paper, rubber and cork. For a good place to hide when being chased by hyenas. Is there a limit to what trees can do? No – science has shown that just looking at trees can help us feel less stressed! Unless, of course, you **ARE** being chased by a hyena.

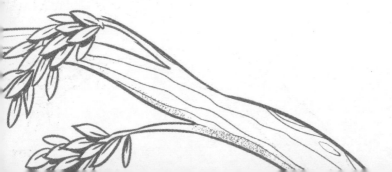

Pick a tree to adopt, either in your garden or near enough to visit weekly. Then just … look. Watch how it changes through the year. Notice which creatures call it home (a single oak tree can boast up to 500 different species!). You haven't adopted just one plant – but an entire **ECOSYSTEM**!

10 WAYS TO MAKE YOUR TREE FEEL LOVED

1 Hug it.

2 Climb it (if it's safe and appropriate – and always ask an adult to supervise).

3 Measure it. Standing a few hundred metres away, hold out your hand so it looks like you're pinching your tree with your thumb at the base of the trunk and your forefinger at the very top of the crown. Carefully turn your hand, keeping your fingers the same space apart, until your forefinger is in line with the ground (but your thumb is still at the base of the trunk). Note the spot marked by your forefinger, then measure the actual distance between that spot and the trunk to find the height of your tree.

4 Identify it. Use clues like the shape and size of leaves and compare them with pictures in a book.

5 Preserve it. Take leaf rubbings, or collect and press leaves between sheets of newspaper and cardboard.

6 Frame it. Take a picture of the tree each week from the same spot. You could go digital too – turn the pics into a time-lapse clip showing how the tree changes over the year.

7 Art it. Create natural art using materials from your tree, such as fallen leaves, needles, twigs, keys or pine cones.

8 Science it. Hunt for microhabitats and find out who's hiding there. Try cracks in the bark, holes between roots, the underside of leaves and inside any unsightly bulges known as galls!

9 Clone it. Take cuttings from your tree (if you have permission from the owner) and give them as gifts.

10 Plant it. For extra eco-points, plant a tree of your own.

CHALK IT UP

Twenty-first century people have a bad habit of buying more 'stuff' as soon as we feel bored. But instead of always looking for the new, try revisiting the past …

What did we do for fun in a world before plastic dart guns, plastic paddling pools and plastic sports equipment? Ok, so hoop trundling or playing football with a pig's bladder probably aren't going to catch on anytime soon, but some of the old ideas are worth revisiting – especially as they tend to be more environmentally friendly.

PLANET-O-METER

Chalk, for example. Chalk is a natural material, made from gypsum or limestone. This means it can be used outside without harming wildlife. It creates little waste, as it all gets used up, and it often has simple recyclable packaging. Invest in a packet of coloured chalks and you can create your own fun without reaching for a new toy ...

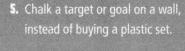

COUNTDOWN
TO CALCIUM
CARBONATE FUN

5. Chalk a target or goal on a wall, instead of buying a plastic set.

4. Chalk enormous versions of board games on a driveway or patio.

3. Use chalk to lay an eco-friendly treasure trail in the garden.

2. Paint a section of wall or a piece of furniture with eco-friendly blackboard paint. Chalk reminders and lists instead of using paper.

1. Mix chalk and water and paint your own (temporary) mural.

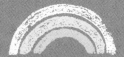

DON'T

**DOODLE IN CHALK ON
PUBLIC PAVEMENTS
OR WALLS – THIS
IS ILLEGAL IN SOME
COUNTRIES.**

TAKE A BAG FOR A WALK

When is a plastic bag not an eco-villain? When it swaps sides and helps to rid the world of litter!

PLANET-O-METER

Litter is bad news for wildlife. It also looks disgusting, and quickly turns beautiful scenes into no-go zones … which encourages people to drop even more litter!

The main things dropped by litterbugs in the UK are confectionery wrappers, soft drinks cans, bottles and lids, and fast-food packaging. Obviously, one of the easiest ways you can help is by not being a litterbug yourself. But you can have an even bigger impact by helping to clear up after the 62 per cent of the population (that's almost two in every three people!) who admit to dropping litter.

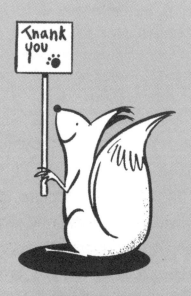

Tidying up nature is a lot more fun than tidying your bedroom! You can wear cool kit, use a mechanical grabber or even combine it with a treasure hunt. So the next time a plastic bag makes its way into your house, take it on a walk. It could be a stroll in the park, a woodland wander, or just a five-minute dash around a patch of land near your home. Aim to fill the bag with litter. Each piece you pick up could stop a bird choking on a balloon, a shrew suffocating in a plastic bag, or a hedgehog getting its head stuck in a container. This kind of tidying up can save lives!

More than 2 million pieces of litter are dropped in the UK every day. This is even more shocking when you think that littering is a criminal offence in the UK and can be punished with a fine - or worse.

COUNTDOWN
TO A LITTER BLITZ

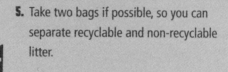

5. Take two bags if possible, so you can separate recyclable and non-recyclable litter.

4. Bend old wire coat hangers into a diamond shape and use them to hold your bags open.

3. Look out for opportunities to join a group litter-picking event, or to join in with a virtual event such as #2MinuteBeachClean. It's fun to share your haul!

2. Recycle as much of the litter as you can (this is MUCH easier if you separate the litter as you go).

1. Stay safe – read the tips on the next page.

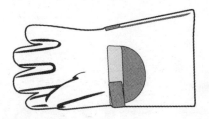

STAYING SAFE

Never go litter picking on your own – always take at least one adult with you (they're also handy for carrying the rubbish!). Wear protective clothing, bright clothes and tough gloves (gardening gloves are great for this). Never pick up broken glass. Report fly tipping, or any needles you come across, to your local police and if you find them, stop collecting in that area. Choose a safe location to litter pick, and avoid roads because you won't be able to look out for traffic at the same time. Afterwards, wash your hands really well with soap and water – even if you used gloves.

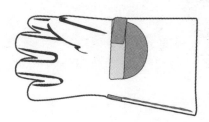

SAY 'NO THANK YOU' CARDS

It's great getting gifts, especially if they're eco-kind (see pages 50–51). But nothing spoils the vibe like feeling guilty for forgetting to write thank-you cards.

PLANET-O-METER

Well, say goodbye to guilt! Every time you don't send a greetings card – from thank-you notes to birthday cards – you're doing the planet a huge favour.

It's not just the paper used to make the cards that's the problem. A whole load of energy and chemicals go into making those brightly coloured pictures, giving them a glossy coating, and gluing on glitter and badges to make them stand out in the shop. And to make matters even worse, many cards are sold in plastic sleeves.

If you must buy cards, look out for those made from sustainable forests or recycled paper. Or, even better, try these alternative ways to show someone you care.

TOP 10 CARD-BUSTING ALTERNATIVES

1 Make a phone call.

2 Send an eCard or video greeting – look out for apps that do this for free!

3 Make your own card using stuff you find around the house.

4 Send a letter or a drawing instead.

5 Send a postcard without an envelope. The envelope glue has an eco-impact too.

6 Write a special message in chalk instead (see pages 104–105).

7 Bake and decorate a cake or some cupcakes – it's cuter (and tastier) than a card.

8 Print a favourite photo and write a message on the back.

9 Take a leaf from the ancient Romans' book and send, er, leaves! They used to exchange branches from olive and laurel trees, but you could give someone a cutting to plant.

10 Save any cards you are sent and reuse the pictures as thank-you notes.

Americans send more greetings cards than anyone else in the world. In the 2010s, they bought 7 billion cards every year, costing $7.5 billion!

EAT MORE CHIPS!

They might seem fairly harmless, sitting quietly in the dark, but potatoes are doing their bit to destroy the planet.

PLANET-O-METER

Potatoes have the tenth biggest carbon footprint of all foods. Every kilogram of potatoes your family eats releases the equivalent of 2.9 kg of carbon dioxide into the atmosphere – more than any other protein-rich plant food.

More than 80 per cent of these emissions are down to the energy and time it takes to cook potatoes. Baking a large potato for an hour is much worse for the environment than cooking oven chips for 20 minutes.

So eat more chips – science says so!

COTTON ON TO CLOTHES WASTE

PLANET-O-METER

From sports kits to souvenirs to your school uniform, there are bound to be a few cotton T-shirts hanging out in your wardrobe. Don't ignore them – they're slowly destroying the planet.

Cotton comes from plants, so it must be better for the environment than synthetic clothes, right? Not necessarily. Cotton is one of the most high-maintenance crops in the world – imagine the Kardashians AND the Royal Family in plant form, and you'll get the picture. It takes 2,700 litres of water to make a single cotton T-shirt. That's enough drinking water to keep a person alive for nearly 2.5 **YEARS**. Cotton production also uses more pesticides than any other single crop. That's a vat of chemicals dumped on the land just so that someone can wear a slogan tee.

Cotton doesn't stop being thirsty once it's in your wardrobe, either. In the UK, we wear denim jeans an average of two or three times before we wash them. That adds up to 750 litres of water to wash just one pair of jeans over its lifetime.

We also need to stop thinking of cotton as disposable. From sports teams you no longer play for, to that stain that won't come out, or the tie-dye T-shirt that you'd rather die than wear in public … you're bound to have at least one piece of cotton clothing you no longer wear but can't donate or swish (see pages 72–75). Find another way to stop that cotton going to waste. Try these ideas on for size.

GLUG GLUG GLUG

COUNTDOWN TO A LONGER LIFE FOR COTTON

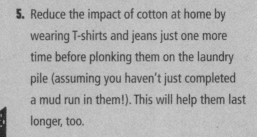

5. Reduce the impact of cotton at home by wearing T-shirts and jeans just one more time before plonking them on the laundry pile (assuming you haven't just completed a mud run in them!). This will help them last longer, too.

4. Avoid tumble-drying and ironing cotton clothes to reduce their carbon footprint.

3. Cotton jersey doesn't fray. If you've outgrown a T-shirt or just got bored of it, try cutting a new neckline or sleeves. Et voilà! A brand new top!

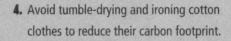

2. Cut old cotton into long strips, plait them together, and you've got an instant hairband, belt or pet toy.

1. Look up instructions for making pompoms and use cotton strips instead of wool. You only need scissors, scrap cardboard and the ability to tie a knot. String your pompoms together to make garlands, decorate an old cushion with them, or even use them to replace sponges.

3.6 billion clothes are sitting unworn in the UK's wardrobes. That's a **massive 57 items each!** Meanwhile, 29 million tonnes of new cotton are produced every year. That's the equivalent of **29 T-shirts** for every **single person** on the planet.

TAKE YOUR JUNK FOR A HOT CHOCOLATE ...

… at a repair café! And if you can't find one, start your own.

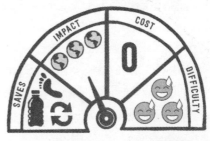

PLANET-O-METER

Think twice before you ditch anything with a battery or a plug. The United Nations has warned that electronic waste, or e-waste, is a MAJOR threat to the environment and to human health. But we still generate around 50 million tonnes of it every year.

This mountain of mobile phones, laptops, TVs, electrical toys, hair straighteners, fairy lights, e-readers and lamps is packed full of valuable materials including gold, silver, copper and platinum. It's more like jewels than junk! No single item is going to look like a glittering treasure chest if you open it up, but together the e-waste thrown away in a single year contains materials worth £40 billion that could be recovered and reused. Yet just 20 per cent of this potential gold (silver, copper and platinum) mine is being recycled.

We also throw away piles of things that could be fixed, which is where repair cafés come in. There are more than 1,500 repair cafés around the world, run by volunteers who can help you to bring broken stuff back to life – for free! Their aim is to reduce the amount of waste going to landfills and the carbon footprint of buying new stuff.

Repair cafés aren't just for electronic items – anything from bicycles and soft toys to jeans and jewellery can be mended while you relax with a hot drink. You'll learn new skills yourself, too, so you can pass the knowledge on.

Visit
REPAIRCAFE.ORG
to see if there is one in your area.
If not, ask your school or youth group
if you can start your own. Your local
council may also be willing to help.

DRAUGHTBUSTERS

MIND THE GAP

PLANET-O-METER

**There's something strange in your neighbourhood.
It's silent and invisible, but gives you goosebumps and
sends a shiver down your spine. Who you gonna call?
Draughtbusters!**

Draughts may be small, but they can add up to a house-sized problem.
Even the tiniest of gaps can let warm air leak out of our homes, and
cold air flows in to take its place. This lowers the room temperature,
meaning the boiler has to burn more fuel. Draughts also make us feel
colder than we really are, tempting us to turn up the heating.

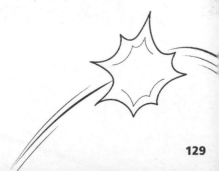

It can be fun to hunt for draughts. Wait for a cold day (a breeze makes it even easier), then hold a feather near one of these Draught Danger Zones:

☆ external doors

☆ key holes

☆ letter box

☆ loft hatch

☆ cellar door

☆ unused chimneys

☆ windows

☆ cat flaps

☆ gaps between floorboards

☆ gaps under skirting boards

☆ behind bath panels

☆ anywhere pipes leave the house

If you feel the flow of cold air or see your feather flutter, take action. You can buy draught excluders, but it's just as easy to fill small gaps with rolled-up newspaper. For larger gaps, try stuffing one leg of an old pair of tights or skins with fabric or paper scraps to make a draught excluder. A rolled-up rug or blanket will also work a treat. You'll be reusing waste materials, too! Plug the gaps and you should be able to turn the heating down and save on energy bills. Great news for your novelty jumper fund (see pages 140–141).

> **Don't get too good at gap-filling and cover up air vents, such as air bricks, extractor fans, or trickle vents. They do an important job letting fresh air circulate.**

WHOOSH!

THINK LIKE A
SEA TURTLE

What's the difference between a plastic bag and a jellyfish? It's no joke. Turtles really can't tell the difference, and their mistake is costing them their lives.

PLANET-O-METER

Plastic carrier bags are used for an average of 12 minutes. So it's totally sensible to make them from plastic designed to last 500 years. Right?*

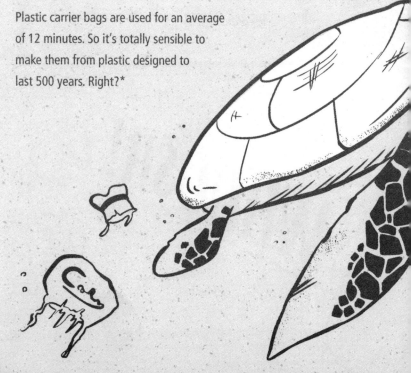

*Did you spot the error in this logic? Congratulations, that puts you one step ahead of most of the world's population. Up to 1 trillion single-use plastic bags are used around the world each year – that's nearly **2 MILLION** every minute!

Each bag is the start of a sad story. Around 8 million tonnes of plastic end up in the world's oceans every year. Smaller animals get trapped inside plastic bags and suffocate. Large animals don't fare much better. A shark or seal has no hands to remove a carrier bag from around its neck. If a plastic bag blocks a fish's gills, the fish can no longer breathe oxygen from the water and suffocates.

Marine animals are eating more and more plastic. One study of seabirds found that 9 in 10 had plastic in their stomachs, and not just a little bit – more than 36 pieces per bird! Turtles and beaked whales are known to eat plastic bags, mistaking them for jellyfish or squid. Even non-predatory filter-feeding whales are swallowing plastic bags that drift into their enormous mouths. Globally, up to a million seabirds and 100,000 marine mammals and sea turtles die each year from eating plastic.

The bad news? We are all responsible for the problem. The good news? We can all help to solve it. Small changes add up to a BIG difference. Take a cloth bag or a rucksack with you every time you head for the shops. Carry snacks in reusable boxes instead of food bags. Next time a shop asks 'Would you like a bag?', channel your inner sea turtle and say no.

Governments around the world have introduced bans or fees to limit plastic bag use, and they really work. Even a small charge can make a big difference. Before a fee was introduced in Britain, the average person used around 140 bags per year. In just one year, this fell to around 25 bags per year. But we can do better than this. In Denmark, where plastic bags have been taxed for more than 25 years, people use an average of just four bags per year.

GET ON YOUR BIKE
(OR SKATES,
OR SCOOTER ...)

Every time you grab a lift in a car, the exhaust fumes leave an invisible trail of greenhouse gases and other unpleasant things in your wake.

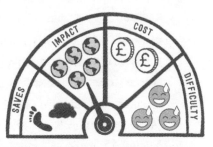

PLANET-0-METER

These include toxic gases such as carbon monoxide, as well as tiny particles and droplets of hundreds of different chemicals. Some of these particles are so small, you could line up 10 widthways across a single human hair (if you had really tiny tweezers). There's no way to avoid breathing them in, and over time they get lodged in our lungs and can seriously damage our health. Children are most at risk because your lungs are still growing.

This type of air pollution is such a serious issue that in some places idling (leaving the engine running while a vehicle is not moving) is against the law. Experiments have shown that staying inside the car doesn't help – in fact, air in the back seat of a car is up to 12 times more polluted than the air outside. This is because the car's ventilation system sucks in fumes from the road outside, trapping them inside the car.

One solution is to drive less and walk or cycle more. Start by keeping a diary of every car journey you make for a week, including lifts from other people. Which could you have made on two wheels (or two feet!) if you'd set off a bit earlier? Swap in at least one walk or bike ride next week, and you'll be making a difference.

Although 42 per cent of people in the UK own a bike, two-thirds of us cycle less than once a year, or never. The average British child only makes 13 cycle trips per year.

On your BIKE!

Stay safe. Get your bike checked to make sure it's roadworthy. Always wear bright or reflective clothes and a helmet when cycling. Cross roads carefully. Use lights after dusk.

DRESS TO IMPRESS

It's the easiest challenge in this book. You're probably doing it already!

PLANET-O-METER

Every time you hear a radiator or air-conditioning unit crank up, try to think of it as a boring-looking T-Rex. Heating and cooling our homes gobbles up energy faster than you can say triceratops, and most of this energy still comes from fossil fuels – either directly or to make electricity.

If you're feeling too hot or too cold at home, visit your wardrobe before you head for the thermostat. In cold weather, put on a jumper or a fleece – they're not just for outside! In warm weather, peel layers off before you decide to switch on the air-conditioning.

There are other easy things you can do, too. Don't dry wet clothes and towels on radiators. This lowers the room temperature and makes the boiler work harder. Put a rack near the radiator instead. Keep your curtains and furniture away from the radiator too, and close your blinds or curtains as it starts to get dark, to stop heat escaping.

If you're feeling super keen, why not check if your heating system is wearing a jumper too? Wrapping insulation around hot water tanks and exposed pipes will keep water hotter for longer, giving your boiler a break. (Use foam insulation rather than a knitted number). It's an easy way to cut energy use and bills. Just think – you could use that extra money to buy a nice fluffy jumper!

APPOINT YOURSELF FAMILY CHIEF ...

... of recycling.
(Everyone has to
start somewhere.)

PLANET-O-METER

Your mission, if you
choose to accept it, is to
keep everyone away from
the bin. There are two ways you could do this. **1)** By dropping in
some raw fish or ripe cheese on a hot day. Effective, but it won't
improve the kitchen environment. Or **2)** Do your homework,
research what can and can't be recycled in your area and
stick up reminders absolutely **EVERYWHERE**.

COUNTDOWN TO WASTE DOMINATION

5

Track how many bin bags your family puts out for each collection for a month, and see if you can get the number down.

4

List all the types of rubbish your family throws away: metal, compostable waste, glass, plastic, cooked food, card, batteries ... The easiest way to do this is to stick a tally chart by the bin.

3

Work through the list and identify where your family could be better at recycling. Then tell them if they really love you, they'll want to protect the planet that they are passing on to you by following your new rules.

MWAH HAH HAH HA

MWAH HAH HAH HA

2

Make sure there is a small bin in the kitchen for fruit and veg scraps, coffee grounds and tea bags. Use the contents to start a compost heap (see page 65).

MWAH HAH HAH HA

MWAH HAH HAH HA

1

Put a cardboard box next to the bin to collect paper that's only been used on one side. Then transfer it to the printer.

DESIGN YOUR DREAM DEN

Upcycling is a great way to create a special space without costing the Earth (or all your pocket money).

PLANET-O-METER

When we think about being energy efficient at home, saving heat and electricity springs to mind (see pages 81–83 and 140–141). But all your 'stuff' has a carbon footprint, too.

From furniture to fairy lights, beanbags to board games, we all like to surround ourselves with nice things. And just like clothes, our tastes keep changing. No teenager wants (or fits) the same furniture they had as a toddler!

Each year, Britons alone throw out more than 1.6 million tonnes of furniture and other bulky waste. That's the weight of **88 MILLION** single mattresses. Even a princess couldn't feel a pea through that lot!

Most of this bulky waste is burned or buried in landfills. But furniture has great reuse potential. In fact, a study showed that **HALF** of the bulky waste sent to landfill in that UK could be reused. This would also reduce the demand for new furniture.

Upcycling gives you the best of both worlds. You can turn old furniture or junk-shop finds into something amazing that looks brand-new and 100 per cent you.

TOP 10 EASY
UPCYCLING PROJECTS

1 Paint all or part of a piece of furniture with eco-friendly blackboard paint to create a surface you can doodle on.

2 Use Japanese washi tape to add colour and pattern to old furniture. It covers up dents and scratches, and it's made from sustainable natural fibres like rice and bamboo.

3 Use another Japanese export – origami – to make decorations. From colourful cranes to terrifying tarantulas, you can fold scrap paper into whatever floats your (paper) boat.

4 Look out for second-hand stools or office chairs. It's surprisingly easy to add a brand-new cover using some of your favourite fabric and a staple gun.

5 Look out for 'junk' that can be used in different ways. A plant pot or wire rubbish bin turned upside down might make a great bedside table.

6 Buy pictures from charity shops, paint the frames in bright colours and create your own gallery.

7 Use wallpaper to update an old chest of drawers or wardrobe. It's not just for walls!

8 Instead of chucking an old lampshade, remove the fabric cover, paint the metal frame and fit a low-wattage light bulb.

9 Frame a single page from a monthly planner, and you can write on it again and again with wipeable pen.

10 Hang a piece of string and use wooden clothes pegs to display photos.

GO ROUND AND ROUND IN CIRCLES

7.6 billion people in the world means 15.2 billion feet! Use yours to kick waste off the agenda.

PLANET-O-METER

Most things we buy move in a straight line. Think about it:

RAW MATERIAL → *FACTORY* → *SHOP* → *YOUR HOME* → *DISPOSAL*

If something stops working, we replace it. In fact, many products are designed on purpose to fail after a certain amount of time or to be difficult to repair. Computer chips make it easy to programme a limited lifespan. This helps the economy because it makes sure people keep coming back to the shops to buy more and more items. But it's terrible for the planet.

So, what if the straight line is bent into a circle instead?

This is known as the circular economy. Businesses still make money, and people still get paid – but waste is eliminated. It means planning ahead so that reuse and recycling are built into product design. It means encouraging customers to return used or broken products, so that the materials can be recovered and new versions don't have to be made from scratch. Look out for signs of the circular economy popping up near you – including shops that pay you to bring back bottles and cans for recycling, or that give you a discount if you return used clothes to reuse, resell or recycle.

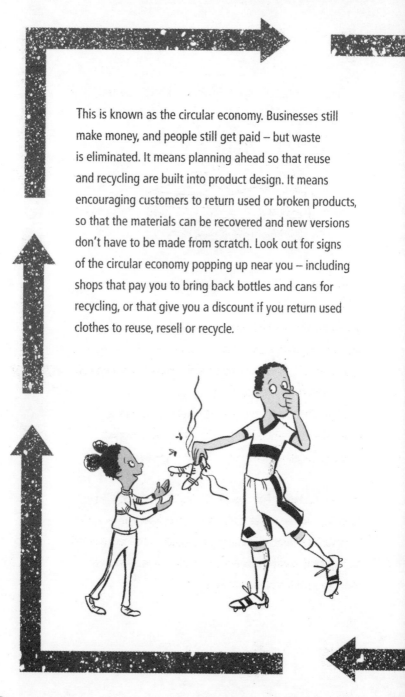

Some of the most exciting plans involve sports shoes. More than 20 billion pairs of shoes are produced every year around the world, and less than 5 per cent of these are ever recycled. Projects like Sport Infinity are trying to change this by creating sports shoes that will never end up in the bin. Imagine football boots made out of an inexhaustible 3D super-material. After your favourite footballer has finished with them, every gram can be broken down and remoulded to make new boots – for you!

It might be some time before you find Messi's recycled boots on your feet, but in the meantime, look out for sports shoes made of recycled materials – such as trainers created from plastic waste collected on beaches in the Maldives! You can save the planet in style.

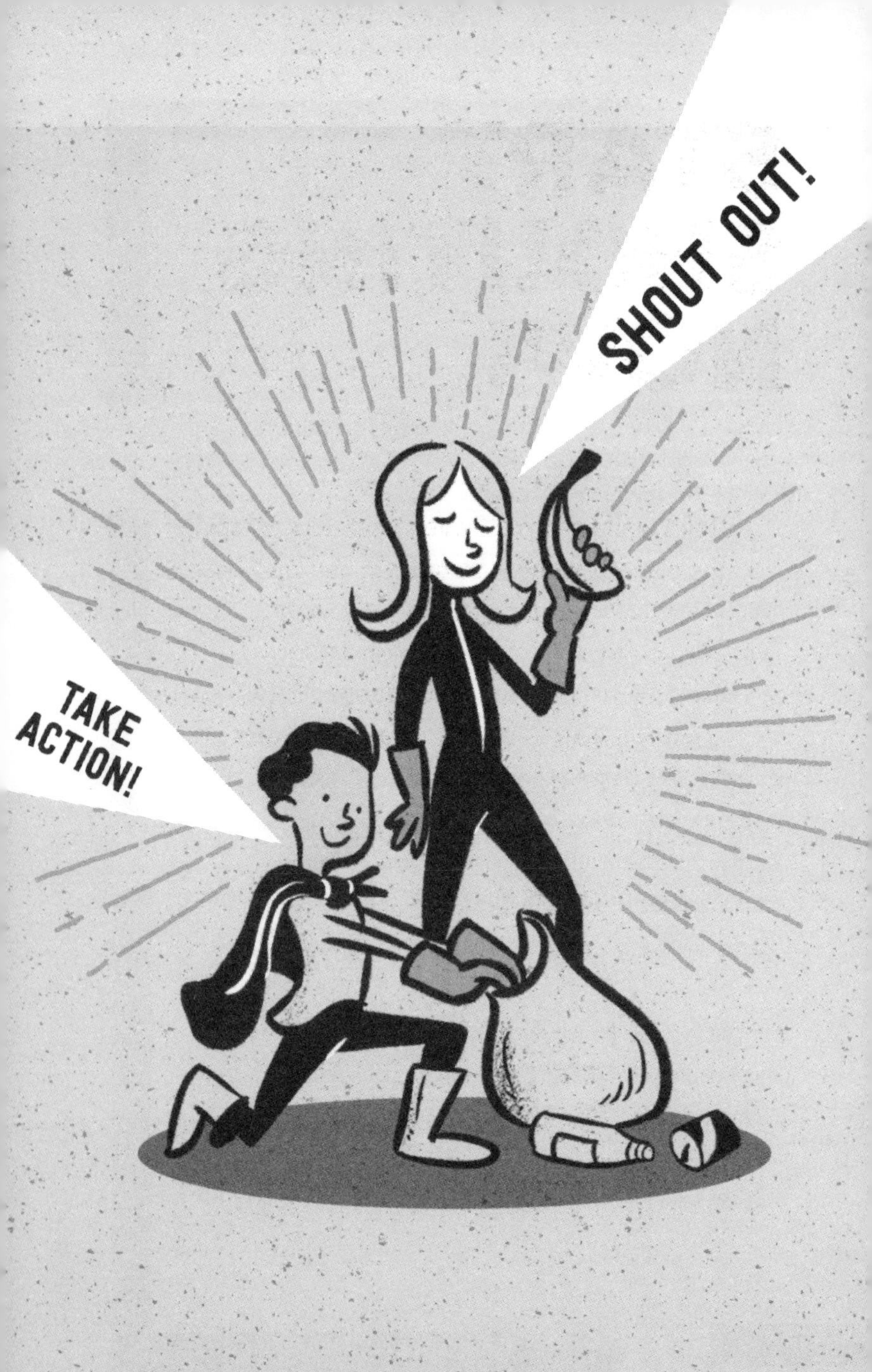
SHOUT OUT!
TAKE ACTION!

START SHOUTING NOW!

Don't wait until you leave school to start saving the planet – it might be too late. You can become a campaigner right now.

Get ready to meet some amazing kids who have taken action to tackle some of our biggest global problems.

PLANET-O-METER

FELIX FINKBEINER started campaigning to plant a million trees when he was just nine years old. Today, 10 years later, he runs an organisation called Plant for the Planet and has recruited more than 67,000 young 'climate justice ambassadors' from all over the globe. Having smashed his original target, Felix is now aiming to get a trillion trees planted around the world!

Join Felix's team:

PLANT-FOR-THE-PLANET.ORG/EN/JOIN-IN/BECOME-AN-AMBASSADOR

ANN MAKOSINSKI began inventing when she was seven. After creating a torch that gets its energy from body heat and a mug that can charge a phone, she began winning awards and giving talks around the world – all in her teens!

ANNMAKOSINSKI.COM

XIUHTEZCATL MARTINEZ first started campaigning for the environment when he was six. He's organised more than 100 events around the world, and was one of the youngest people ever to speak on a United Nations panel. He's also youth director of Earth Guardians. Xiuhtezcatl asks, if you don't step up, who will?

XIUHTEZCATL.COM/MY-STORY

ELLA and **AMY MEEK** were shocked when they discovered how badly plastic affects life below water. They set out to pick up 100,000 pieces of plastic litter, but also founded Kids Against Plastic to shout about the problems with single-use plastic. They are looking out for more children to join the KidsVPlastic Crew and fight for the planet.

CLEARPLASTICUK.NET

Are you feeling inspired? You could join an existing campaign, or take the lead and start something new. A campaign to ban plastic water bottles from your school? Or to make everyone walk to school? A campaign to clean up litter in your local area? This book might give you ideas, but it's not the boss of you, so be your own eco-hero!

ONCE YOU'VE DECIDED WHAT TO FOCUS ON, TRY THESE THREE THINGS:

☆ Raise funds by running events, such as a sponsored activity, selling things you've made or selling tickets to a show.

☆ Get attention from people in power. They are in a position to change rules and laws. They are also elected to represent **YOUR** voice, so write to them or ask an adult to help you arrange a meeting, and tell them what you think.

☆ Get your campaign in the news. Every time you organise an event or achieve something awesome, ask an adult to help you shout about it to the local press. Send a press release to newspapers, local radio and TV, and children's magazines.

ONLY LEAVE
FOOTPRINTS

How many endangered animals can you name?

PLANET-O-METER

Chances are, you didn't manage to list all **13,267** species on the International Union for Conservation of Nature (IUCN) 'Red List'. When we think about animals at risk of extinction, polar bears, rhinos and tigers come to mind. But most are much smaller, and much closer to home.

In the UK, they include water voles, skylarks, natterjack toads, and many types of bumblebees, butterflies and beetles. If we don't take steps to protect our nearest neighbours, they will follow in the (doomed) footsteps of the brown bears, wolves and lynx that used to roam around Britain.

While you can't hop on a plane to the Arctic and personally save a polar bear, you can make a big difference to the life chances of your local wildlife. Just follow these tips whenever you're exploring nature. It's a walk in the park!

COUNTDOWN TO CARING FOR YOUR NEIGHBOURS

5. Carry all your rubbish home, even biodegradable waste food. Anything you leave behind – from apple cores to cake crumbs – can disrupt an ecosystem.

4. Follow marked paths so you don't damage the plants that wildlife depend on.

3. Keep dogs on a lead.

2. Don't pick wildflowers. This is **SO** important that in many places it's against the law.

1. Don't pull bark off trees or carve your name into the bark!

The IUCN's list of endangered animals, known as the 'Red List', is drawn from a survey of only 5 per cent of Earth's living things, so the total number of threatened species is likely to be much higher.

BE A CITIZEN SCIENTIST

What have earthworms, penguins and zombie flies got in common?

PLANET-O-METER

They've all been stared at by citizen scientists! These are people just like you, who are interested in the world and its wildlife. They help researchers to collect or analyse huge amounts of data that not even the brainiest professor could complete on their own.

Citizen science is all about people power. Your observations will help scientists to answer big questions about our planet and teach us how to protect it.

You don't need any training – just curiosity and access to an internet connection (earthworms need not apply). When you join a project, you'll be asked to carry out a specific task. You might be tagging penguins (cute!) or plastic litter (not so cute!) in photographs taken by robots. You might be looking out for honey bees infected by a parasitic fly that turns them into 'zombees'. Or you might be counting earthworms in your garden and logging the results on an app.

New projects start all the time, so you never know what you'll have the chance to do next. Search 'citizen science' or look at the links below.

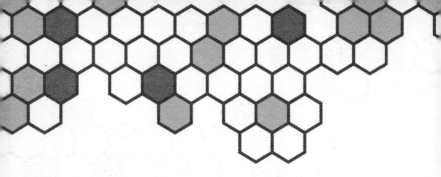

DON'T BEE-LIEVE THE MYTHS

Zombees aside (see page 165), it's not a good time to be a bee.

PLANET-O-METER

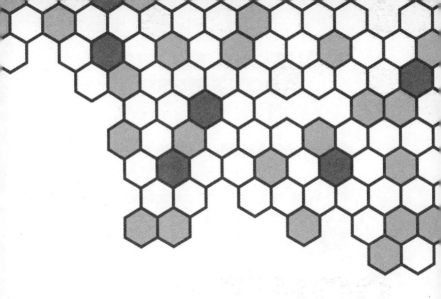

Bees aren't just a source of honey. They pollinate most of the world's flowering plants, including 84 per cent of all the crops that humans eat. Plants don't start growing fruit until they've been pollinated, so without bees and other insects, there would be no chocolate, grapes, strawberries or more than 400 other delicious foods. No Brussels sprouts either, but we'll keep that one quiet.

The work bees do is worth £130 billion to the world's economy, and they do it for free! We're not the only species that depends on bees either. Their hard work props up entire ecosystems all around the world. The scary thing is, the number of wild bees is falling fast. In Europe, nearly 1 in 10 bee species face extinction due to habitat loss, climate change, pesticide poisoning and disease.

BUSTING MYTHS ABOUT BEES

1 THEY'RE ONLY AROUND IN SUMMER.

There are 25,000 different species of bee, and many are active all year round. This means you can help them at any time of year.

2 THEY LIVE IN BIG GROUPS.

Most bees are solitary. They nest on their own, often in holes in the ground. Give them somewhere to nest by leaving patches of bare soil, or building a bug hotel.

3 THEY ONLY LIKE MESSY GARDENS.

Bees would love it if you swapped your lawn for a mini-wildflower meadow (see pages 78–79), but they eat nectar and pollen from many other kinds of flowering plants too. They love large areas of the same flower. Lavender, heather, abelia, mahonia, trees with blossom, trees with catkins and climbing plants like honeysuckle and ivy will bring bees to your garden all year round. Bees will also enjoy foraging from flowers in a vegetable patch – pollinating it for you in the process! If all else fails, just let some of your grass grow longer and encourage clover and dandelions instead of trying to get rid of them.

4 THEY ONLY NEED NECTAR AND POLLEN.

Bees need water too. A bird bath or small pond will help bring bees to your garden.

5 THEY LIKE TO STING.

Most female bees have stings, but solitary bees are not at all aggressive. If you're careful, it's even possible to pet a bumblebee! But never disturb their nests, or they will get grumpy.

BECOME AN ART-ACTIVIST

Could your artwork inspire other people to take action?

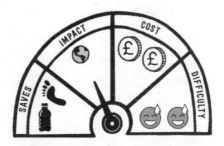

PLANET-O-METER

It's not just scientists who are key to saving the planet. Artists can be just as good at inspiring change. From toxic sludge paintings to grasshopper burgers to 1,600 papier mâché pandas snuggled up under the Eiffel Tower (yes, really), art has the power to make people pay attention to the problems our planet is facing.

You don't have to be a professional artist to get involved. One man from the UK simply collected every single piece of plastic packaging he used in a year and turned them into a giant mural. He took it on a tour of the country, shocking people into using less.

YOU COULD TRY ...

☆ Collecting all the milk bottles your family uses and turning them into a giant flock of plastic birds.

☆ Scooping up leftover emulsion paint and creating a mural (get permission first!) instead of tipping it down the drain.

☆ Gathering plastic bottle tops and lids, and using them to create a giant collage out of circles.

Get your school involved and you'll be able to create something with an even bigger impact. Then ask your local newspaper to feature your creation, to spread the word further.

DITCH THE SCHOOL RUN

Not so fast! Before you donate your school uniform and recycle your exercise books, please note that you *will* still have to go to school! You'll just need to find a better way to get there ...

PLANET-O-METER

Save money and get healthier without even trying. It sounds like a no-brainer – but the number of children walking to school is actually falling!

In the Netherlands, one of our nearest neighbours, around 49 per cent of children cycle to and from school. In the UK, it's just 1 to 3 per cent. So many journeys are made by car that the school run has its own carbon footprint – 2 million tonnes of carbon dioxide every year.

One-third of children are driven less than 1.5 km to the school gates. Are you one of them? If so, changing this habit can make a big difference – not only to the planet but to your future. Walking, cycling, scooting or skating to school leaves you more alert and ready to learn. Children who are more active even do better in tests than children who are driven to school. Not convinced yet? The average family could save £400 a year by doing the school run on foot!

Get other families involved too, and you'll make walking safer for everyone. Ask your school to organise a walking bus, a 'walk once a week' challenge, or a park-and-stride scheme.

In the UK, one in five cars on the road each morning are taking children to school.

READ the LABEL
(AND SAVE A RAINFOREST)

Eating meat and dairy is the fastest way to gobble up resources (see pages 10–14), but not all plants are as innocent as they look.

How often do you look at food labels when you grab a snack? It's the only way to catch these eco-baddies, which are replacing rainforests all around the globe.

PALM OIL is found in around half of all packaged products. Huge areas of rainforest have been burned and cleared for planting oil palms instead. In Malaysia and Indonesia, where most of the world's palm oil comes from, rare rainforest species have been driven into smaller and smaller habitats. Native animals such as the orangutan are on the brink of extinction. But it's hard to avoid palm oil unless you cook everything from scratch. If you're choosing a treat in a shop, look out for products that are RSPO-certified. This means the palm oil they contain is from a sustainable source.

PLANET-O-METER

COCOA is another crop responsible for wrecking rainforests. Most of the world's cocoa comes from West Africa. Even in some 'protected' areas, 90 per cent of the land has been converted to farming cocoa. In Côte d'Ivoire, there were once several hundred thousand elephants, but now just 200–400 survive in the country. It doesn't have to be this way. Cocoa plants can be grown in the shade of taller trees without chopping forests down. When you choose a chocolate bar, look out for a little green frog. This shows that a crop is certified sustainable by the Rainforest Alliance.

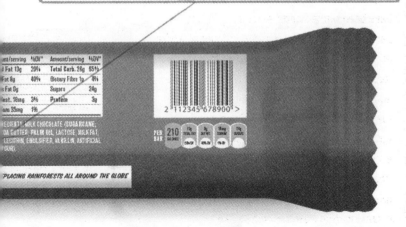

Nutrition Facts	Amount/serving	%DV*	Amount/serving	%DV*
Serving Size 1 Bar	Total Fat 13g	20%	Total Carb. 26g	95%
Calories 210	Sat. Fat 8g	40%	Dietary Fibre 1g	4%
Fat Cal. 110	Trans Fat 0g		Sugars	24g
*Percent Daily Values (DV) are based on a 2000 calorie diet.	Cholest. 10mg	3%	Protein	3g
	Sodium 35mg	1%		

INGREDIENTS: MILK CHOCOLATE (SUGAR, COCOA BUTTER, PALM OIL, LACTOSE, MILK FAT, SOY LECITHIN, EMULSIFIER, VANILLIN, ARTIFICIAL FLAVOUR).

REPLACING RAINFORESTS ALL AROUND THE G

SOYBEANS are a cheap source of protein, vegetable oil and substances that make processed food last longer on the shelf. Produce from soybeans is 'hidden' in around 70 per cent of supermarket products, from bread to chocolate, and is also popular with fast-food chains. Most of the world's soy crops are used to feed farm animals – another reason to cut down on meat (see pages 10–14). Even people who hate soy sauce and avoid edamame beans could be eating around 60 kg of 'hidden' soy every year. It's so popular with food manufacturers that rainforests in South America are rapidly being replaced with soybean plantations.

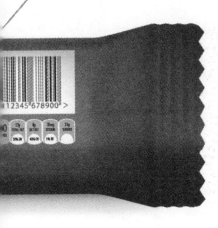

SUGARCANE is grown in more than 100 countries. The end product may be sweet, but the process of making it is not. Long after tropical rainforests are cleared to make way for sugarcane, nearby land and waterways are polluted by chemicals and sludge. It's the opposite of sweet. In fact, it's enough to leave a bitter taste in your mouth.

In South America's Amazon rainforest,
80 trees are cut down every four seconds.
64 of these are cleared to make way for farming.

CACHE IN

You won't need a compass, a map or a spade – just a family member with a smartphone.

Once you've found them and managed to drag their attention from the screen, ask them to download the free geocaching app (see **geocaching.com**). Geocaches are little treasure troves that have been hidden by people all over the world. Once they are logged on to the official website, anyone can use the world's global positioning system (GPS) to track them down.

PLANET-O-METER

Geocaching is addictive and a great way to explore the countryside near your home. As you look closely for caches or clues, you'll notice more wildlife too.

Some caches are big enough to contain actual treasure. When you find one, you can take an item as long as you leave one behind. It's a fun way to reuse plastic gifts from party bags, instead of sending them to landfills.

Always take an adult with you and follow the tips on page 162 to make sure your geocaching walks don't harm wildlife. You can also take part in the 'Cache in, Trash out!' initiative, to leave your trail tidier than you found it. If you decide to get creative and hide your own geocache, follow the tips on geocaching.com to make sure it's environmentally friendly.

GAME OVER

If this book were a video game, this page would be the hardest level. Are you up for the challenge?

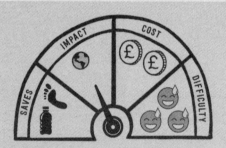

PLANET-O-METER

First the bad news. 91 per cent of you play video games regularly, and the devices you play on are thirsty for energy. In the EU, downloading and playing a typical game releases up to 7.91 kg of carbon dioxide into the atmosphere. This is actually many times bigger than the carbon footprint of buying a game on disk in a shop.

Now the ... actually, there's only bad news. Most of the tips in this book are about finding alternative ways to do the same thing. But the only way to make a difference in video-game land is to download less and play less.

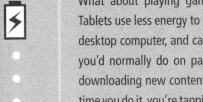

What about playing games on a phone or tablet? Tablets use less energy to run than a console, laptop or desktop computer, and can be a good swap for things you'd normally do on paper (see pages 84–87). But downloading new content still has a big impact. Each time you do it, you're tapping into vast communications and data storage networks that involve energy-hungry 'server farms' and even satellites in space!

In the US, game consoles use an estimated 16 billion kWh of electricity per year – the same as a city of 1.4 million people.

COUNTDOWN TO GAMING THAT WON'T COST THE EARTH

5. Switch devices off at the wall when you have finished playing or downloading.

4. Don't leave your device on for downloads while you are out or asleep.

3. Download games during non-peak times (see pages 81–83).

2. If possible, download games when your device is in standby mode.

1. Think carefully about which games you really want to get, and try not to see them as cheap and disposable.

More than 10 per cent of all
electricity produced around the
world goes on information and
communications technology (ICT).

GET A GREEN PET

Don't worry, you don't have to trade your BFF (best furry friend) for a grasshopper, frog or crocodile.

This is all about taking action to reduce your pet's carbon pawprint. So how big is a carbon pawprint? The answer lies in these sums by a geography professor from UCLA.

Relax, you don't have to do the maths ... the professor has done it for you! He worked out the impact that pet food has on our planet, and

$$F_A = \frac{E_{Dog}^a}{E_{Dog}^a + E_{Cat}^a} \left(P_{Dog,P} \frac{1}{M_{Dog,P}} \sum_{Dog,P} F_A^m + P_{Dog,N} \frac{1}{M_{Dog,N}} \sum_{Dog,N} F_A^m \right)$$

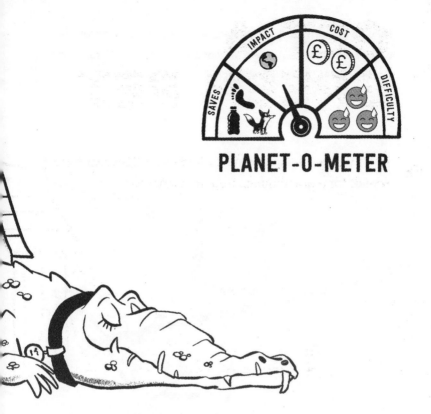

PLANET-O-METER

the answer was scarier than a giant spider. If the 163 million cats and dogs in the USA were to start a nation of their own, it would be the fifth-biggest meat-eating country in the world! Producing meat puts huge pressure on the planet (see pages 10–14) and their meaty diets give these pets the same carbon footprint as 13.6 million cars.

$$+ \; \frac{E^a_{Cat}}{E^a_{Dog} + E^a_{Cat}} \left(P_{Cat,P} \; \frac{1}{M_{Cat,P}} \; \Sigma_{Cat,P} \; F^m_A + P_{Cat,N} \; \frac{1}{M_{Cat,N}} \; \Sigma_{Cat,N} \; F^m_A \right),$$

Pet dogs and cats are also predators, and one of the main threats to wild birds and animals around the world. In the US, cats capture and kill up to 1.4 billion birds and 22.3 billion mammals every year.

There are loads of awesome things about pets too – they're great company, help to get us outside for walks and teach us to be kind to animals. But pets can't change their eco-impact on their own – so it's up to you to help them. If you already live with a dog or a cat, you can reduce their carbon footprint by looking out for eco-friendly pet foods, and avoiding food made from beef and fish. Keep dogs on a lead when you're outdoors and fit a bell or sonar device to your cat's collar, to make it harder for them to hunt wildlife.

If you're thinking about giving a home to a new pet, rodents, fish and chickens are greener choices. Chickens eat waste fruit and veg from your kitchen, converting it into eggs you can eat – and are **MUCH** cuter than a compost heap!

Up to 987 million dogs and 752 million cats are kept as pets around the world.

EAT SLOW

Cutting down on fast food is a short cut to saving the planet.

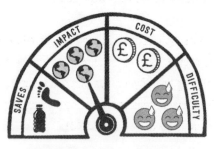

PLANET-O-METER

Fast food is fast harming the planet in lots of ways. It tends to use lots of meat. It often involves a car journey to buy a single meal. And each item you order comes in its own packaging, from cups with straws to tiny plastic tubs of sauce. One popular fast-food chain has 37,000 restaurants around the world, but only 10 per cent of them do any recycling.

The same company have said they'll stop using polystyrene foam containers but have given themselves a deadline that is years in the future. Imagine how popular you'd be if you agreed to tidy your bedroom ... in 2,000 days' time!

If fast-food restaurants aren't prepared to act quickly when it comes to saving the planet, at least you can. Next time you fancy a treat, try making one of your favourite fast foods at home. It's quick and easy, and science tells us that foods that are good for the planet are also more likely to be good for **YOU**.

INSTEAD OF GOBBLING NACHOS AT THE CINEMA ...

Ask an adult to snip a couple of plain wheat tortilla wraps into random pieces using scissors. Lay them out on a baking tray and ask your helper to pop them in a moderately hot oven for 10 minutes. Scatter over grated cheese, sliced green chillies and mayonnaise.

INSTEAD OF POPPING OUT FOR FRIED CHICKEN ...

Ask an adult to cut some chicken breasts or thighs into bite-sized chunks. Dip them into a bowl of beaten egg, then a bowl of flour, then finally a bowl of breadcrumbs mixed with salt, pepper and a sprinkle of paprika if you have it. Ask your helper to put them in a hot oven for 20–25 minutes until they are golden brown and cooked through. Eat with dips or in a burger bun.

INSTEAD OF GRABBING A CONE OF FRIES ...

Ask an adult to cut a butternut squash or some sweet potatoes into wedges (no need to peel them first – just scrub). Pop them on a baking tray and drizzle over a little bit of oil and some salt and pepper. Ask your helper to put them in a hot oven for about 20 minutes, until they're soft, sweet and super delicious!

INSTEAD OF ORDERING PIZZA ...

Make your own! It's really easy to make a flatbread base –
add three mugs of self-raising flour, one mug of water, two
tablespoons of oil and a sprinkle of salt to a bowl and mix really
well with your hands. When you've got a squidgy dough, divide
it into four balls. Roll one of the balls into a flat circle (or oval – it
doesn't have to be perfect) and add your favourite toppings.
Then ask your adult helper to pop it in a hot oven for 10 minutes,
until the crust is golden brown. You can keep spare balls of
dough in the fridge for a couple of days.

INSTEAD OF BUYING A BAG OF POPCORN
(WHICH IS MOSTLY PACKAGED AIR!) ...

Tip some corn kernels into a saucepan in a single layer (it might
not look like much, but it will fill the pan with popcorn!). Add a
teaspoon of sunflower oil and stir. Then ask your helper to put
the pan on a medium heat with a lid on. Once you start hearing
pops, give the pan an occasional shake. When the popping stops,
let it cool, sprinkle on a little salt and start munching.

Snack, confectionery and fast-food packaging makes up around 40 per cent of all the world's litter.

SCRUB YOURSELF GREEN

PLANET-O-METER

If you're already taking shorter showers (see page 23), turn over to discover how to make them even greener.

Even the smallest choices have an eco-impact – like liquid soap versus bar soap. Liquid soap takes more energy to make and uses more plastic packaging. It also contains a lot of water, making it heavier to transport. Despite dispensers, we tend to use more liquid soap than we need, meaning more waste.

Swap liquid soap and shower gel for bar soap free from palm oil (see page 180) and packaged in paper. To cut down on waste, save the scraps each time you get near the end of the bar. Grate them and add a little warm (not hot) water to make them squishy. Push the mixture into a mould (any flexible plastic packaging will do) and leave for a few days before you pop your new soap out of the mould.

LIQUID SOAP

BAR SOAP

GET RID OF THIS BOOK

Not via the bin! Remember,

THIS BOOK IS NOT RUBBISH.

It's a book that gives readers the knowledge to make a difference to the local and global environment. Not to mention a really good reason to eat more chips. It can't do all that from your shelf. So once you've put each page into action, spread the word by passing this book on.

Pass it to a friend, family member, neighbour or school library. Pass it to your teacher or headteacher to enlist help with a project. Pass it to a local politician and ask what they are doing to save the planet.

PLANET-O-METER

BECAUSE IT'S YOUR PLANET AND IT NEEDS ALL THE FRIENDS IT CAN GET.

INDEX

A

animal 10, 11, 12, 14, 37, 63, 79, 89, 93, 94, 134, 180, 182, 194
animal, endangered 47, 51, 160, 163

B

bath 22–23, 24, 73, 130
battery 125, 144
bee 163, 165, 168–169, 170–171
beef 7, 14, 194
bin 48, 61, 65, 85, 142, 144–45, 148, 153, 204
biodegradable 37, 55, 162
bread 41, 63, 182, 198, 199

C

car 12, 13, 14, 89, 95, 136–37, 138, 176, 178, 193, 196
carbon dioxide 12, 13, 17, 22, 43, 73, 99, 118, 176, 188
carbon footprint 12, 84, 118, 123, 126, 146, 176, 188, 193, 194
carbon monoxide 137
cards, greetings 32, 33, 36, 51, 114, 115, 116, 117
cardboard 27, 63, 76, 102, 123, 144, 145
cheese 14, 48, 65, 142, 197
climate change 43, 169
clothes 36, 73–73, 74, 75, 76, 77, 113, 121, 123, 124, 139, 140, 146, 152
compost 18, 20, 34, 35, 55, 62, 63, 64, 65, 144, 145, 195
computer 45, 150, 189
cotton 73, 121, 122, 123, 124
cycle 60, 176, 138

E

economy 150, 152, 169
ecosystem 101, 162, 169
electricity 20, 23, 42, 43, 44, 81, 82, 83, 140, 146, 190, 191
energy 21, 23, 43, 44–45, 64, 84, 87, 99, 115, 118, 131, 140, 141, 146, 156, 188, 189, 202
environment 14, 16, 30, 47, 72, 104, 118, 121, 125, 142, 157, 187, 204
extinction 43, 160, 169, 180

F

farm 10–11, 12, 40, 89, 181, 182, 183
fast food 109, 196, 197, 200
fish 14, 28, 31, 37, 134, 142, 194, 195
flower 60, 79, 162, 170
food 18, 33, 39–40, 41, 43, 48, 65, 72, 89, 118, 134, 144, 162, 169, 180, 182
fossil fuel 43, 81, 140
fruit 39, 40, 63, 145, 169, 195
furniture 100, 106, 140, 146–147, 148

G

garden 61, 65, 78–79, 90, 101, 106, 113, 165, 170, 171
greenhouse gas 11, 22, 81, 99, 136
glitter 36–37, 70, 115

H

habitat 11, 89, 100, 103, 169, 180
heating 14, 22, 43, 129, 131, 140, 141
honey 37, 165, 169

I

insect 14, 79, 89, 169

L

landfill 30, 40, 47, 49, 72, 74, 85, 126, 147, 186
litter 26, 52, 60, 108–109, 110, 111, 112, 113, 157, 158, 165, 200

M

meat 10, 11, 12, 14, 65, 180, 182, 193, 196
microplastic 27, 37, 38

O

ocean 12, 26, 27, 31, 36, 37, 38, 43, 52, 134

P

packaging 47, 48, 64, 105, 109, 174, 196, 200, 202
palm oil 180, 202
paper 27, 55, 61, 63, 84–85, 86–87, 100, 106, 115, 131, 145, 148, 189, 202
pet food 192, 194
plant 55, 64, 65, 93, 95, 121, 162, 169, 170, 180, 181
plastic 27, 28, 30, 31, 36, 37, 54, 55, 132, 134, 144, 153, 157
plastic bag 34, 108, 110, 132–33, 134, 135, 186
plastic bottle 26–27, 28–29, 46, 90, 109, 152, 158, 175
pollen 79, 169, 170, 171
pollution 12, 100, 137, 183

R

rainforest 180, 181, 182, 183
recycle 29, 30, 34, 46, 49, 61, 62, 63, 70, 75, 85, 87, 112, 126, 142, 144, 152, 153, 176, 196

renewable 81, 83, 84
repair 74, 125–126, 150
rubbish 26, 34, 40, 46, 48, 49, 51, 60, 63, 64, 74, 85, 86, 105, 113, 126, 144, 148, 146, 147, 150, 152, 162, 187, 202, 204

S

school 28, 49, 59, 60–61, 82, 84, 86, 121, 126, 155, 158, 175, 176–177, 178, 204
shower 22–23, 24, 25, 66, 68, 69, 201
straw 52, 53, 55, 76, 196
supermarket 39, 40, 182

T

T-shirt 121–122, 123, 124
tree 56, 84, 85, 90, 91, 98–101, 102–103, 116, 156, 162, 170, 181, 183
turtle 53, 132, 134
TV 17, 43, 45, 82, 125, 159

V

vegetable 39, 40, 61, 145, 170, 195
vegetarian 10, 14, 37, 65

W

walk 60, 110, 138, 158, 161, 176, 177, 178, 187, 194
water 12, 17, 18, 19, 20, 21, 22–24, 25, 28, 34, 36, 66, 67, 68, 73, 84, 92, 93, 94, 95, 106, 113, 121, 122, 134, 141, 157, 171, 199, 202
wildlife 52, 78, 79, 105, 108, 161, 162, 164, 185, 187, 194
wrapping paper 32, 33, 70, 87

ALSO AVAILABLE FROM WREN & ROOK

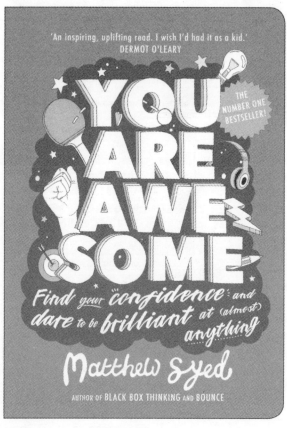

'An inspiring, uplifting read. I wish I'd had it as a kid.'
DERMOT O'LEARY

THE NUMBER ONE BESTSELLER!

YOU ARE AWESOME

Find your "confidence" and dare to be brilliant at (almost) anything

Matthew Syed

AUTHOR OF BLACK BOX THINKING AND BOUNCE

978 1 5263 6115 8 | £9.99